STANDING up for JESUS

CHILDREN'S OBJECT LESSONS

WESLEY T. RUNK

C.S.S. Publishing Company
Lima, Ohio

STANDING UP FOR JESUS

5809/ISBN 0-89536-725-4
PRINTED IN U.S.A.

TABLE OF CONTENTS

Foreword

What child doesn't love to hear a story?

These short "parables-from-life" are based on Gospel scripture texts, and are designed to be presented by the pastor or a worship leader, either at the worship service or at Sunday church school, vacation Bible school, or children's worship time. Each makes use of some common, everyday items.

None of the messages are intended to be presented just as they are written. In fact, none of us *talk* the way we *write*. The storyteller will want to read the Scripture text and the story and (if necessary) rehearse it, until it can be presented in a natural story-telling way.

Often tellers of children's messages forget that they are speaking, *not to the adults* who also happen to be present (even though the adults properly are "overhearing" everything), but that first and primarily the message is a message *to the children* who are gathered in the chancel, or wherever the story is being told. The story-teller will want to be certain that the youngest child who comes to listen can understand what is being said. If eyes and hands begin to stray, make it simpler still (and, perhaps, be prepared to depart from your "learned script" long enough to regain every youngster's attention).

Now, get ready to invite the youngsters, and to say, "Good morning, boys and girls . . ."

Saved in the Nick of Time

Matthew 2:13-18

After they were gone, an angel of the Lord appeared to Joseph in a dream. "Get up and flee to Egypt with the baby and his mother," the angel said, "and stay there until I tell you to return, for King Herod is going to try to kill the child." (v. 13)

Objects: *Some stones, clubs, swords, and knives.*

Good morning, boys and girls. Today I must tell you an awful story and one that we should never forget. It is the story of how a lot of babies were killed by a very jealous king. It is also a story about Jesus and God's plan to save him from death as a baby.

King Herod, the King of Israel at the time of Jesus' birth, was a very jealous king who heard that a baby had been born in Bethlehem who was going to be a king. Now, kings were always afraid that someone else was going to take their place, so they kept large armies around them to protect them from any danger. But, when Herod heard that this king was only a baby, he decided he would kill the child now, and never have to worry about him later. He sent soldiers to Bethlehem and told them to kill every boy child who was two years old and younger. The soldiers did not like the king's order, but they were soldiers, so they went to Bethlehem to do what they were told. God knew of Herod's evil plan and he sent an angel in a dream to Joseph and told Joseph to take Jesus and Mary and travel to Egypt as fast as they could go. Joseph woke Mary, bundled the baby Jesus, and went into Egypt.

Meanwhile, the soldiers came to Bethlehem and carried out the king's orders. With swords, knives, rocks, and clubs they killed every boy baby they could find. It was awful. No one will ever forget it. God will never forget it and he reminds us with this day every year. December 28th is the day that the Church remembers all of the children that were killed by Herod. Of course, he did not kill the one whom he had wanted to kill. Joseph, Mary, and Jesus escaped to Egypt and lived there until Herod died. After Herod died, the holy family of God came back to Nazareth to live.

Murder is a terrible sin. The murder of children, like the little boys in Bethlehem is horrible. But God remembers these children, and he asks us to remember them today. Jesus lived and finally died for all of our sins, even the sins of Herod.

Maybe, when you think about Jesus today, you will remember the children who gave their lives so that Jesus could live to teach us and help us to know God. Amen.

When Things Seem Backwards

Matthew 3:13-17

John didn't want to do it. "This isn't proper," he said. "I am the one who needs to be baptized by you." (v. 14)

Objects: *A father and a son. The father has a school book, a basketball, and wears a stocking cap. The son has a briefcase, a checkbook, and a dress hat.*

Good morning, boys and girls. Today we are going to be a little silly, but I know you will get the point I want you to understand if you go along with me. I have asked Mr. ..... and his son, ..., to help me this morning. I want you to notice anything that you think is strange or not proper about them. Most of us like things to be proper. That means we do things in the right way, the way they should be done. If something is a little different or strange, we say that it is not proper.

Let's take a look at our father and son. Tell me if you see anything that is not quite proper. (Bring out the father wearing the stocking cap with a basketball under one arm and a child's school book under the other. The son should have on his father's hat, a checkbook in one hand, and the briefcase in the other.) If you see anything that does not look proper, call it out and let's see if we all agree. (Give them a few minutes to identify the objects.)

Does it seem proper to you that a man should have a school book, wear a stocking cap, and carry a basketball? Is it proper for a boy to have a briefcase, checkbook, and wear a businessman's hat? It doesn't seem proper, does it? (Let them answer.)

That is kind of the way John the Baptist felt one day when Jesus asked John to do something for him. Let me tell you a little bit about it. Jesus came to the Jordan River where John the Baptist was preaching and baptizing people. He asked John to baptize him. John was surprised and very embarrassed. Did Jesus ask John to baptize him? It wasn't proper. John thought he himself should be baptized by Jesus because Jesus was the Son of God.

What do you do when the Son of God asks you to baptize him? There was only one thing to do. He told Jesus that it wasn't proper and that he could not do it. But Jesus was not concerned about what seemed proper. Jesus wanted to do what was right in the eyes of the people, and he wanted all to know that he agreed with what John the Baptist was saying about getting right with God. He told John that he would have to baptize him whether he thought it was proper or not. John could not very well say no to the Son of God. If Jesus insisted, then he would do it, and Jesus did insist.

That is the way it happened one day in Israel when John tried to keep things proper, and Jesus did something that didn't seem proper, but something that made a lot of people happy.

Don't Give In

Matthew 4:1-11

Jesus said to him, "Again it is written, 'You shall not tempt the Lord your God.' " (v. 7)

Objects: *Some empty pop cans or bottles.*

Good morning, boys and girls. How many of you like to drink pop? What is your favorite kind? (Let them answer.) Do you like to drink it out of the bottle or the can? How would you rather drink it, from a glass or out of the bottle or can? (Let them answer.) Most kids would like to drink it out of the bottle or can. But now let me ask you the big question for today. What do you do with your bottle or can when you are finished with it? Are you tempted to be a polluter? Do you know what a polluter is? (Let them answer.) That's right. A polluter is someone who throws trash just anywhere. I know that you aren't tempted to be a polluter when you drink a bottle of pop in the house, but what about when you drink it outside? Everywhere I go I see empty pop bottles and cans. Someone is really polluting the earth with empty bottles and cans. There is a great temptation to pollute the world with these things. I even see people driving through town in their cars and throwing out empty cans rather than putting them into litter bags. It must be a terrible temptation to throw a can or bottle. Are any of you polluting the earth with these cans or bottles? (Let them answer.) I am glad that you avoid the temptation.

Temptation is a terrible thing. I suppose that you heard

the story about when the Devil tried to tempt Jesus. Three different times the Devil tried to get Jesus to do things his way for a reward, rather than to follow the way of God. He promised Jesus almost anything if Jesus would just worship him, the Devil, rather than God. It was quite a temptation. He promised Jesus that he could fill His hungry body with food if He would worship the Devil. He promised Jesus that he could be a hero if He would worship the Devil, and he also promised Him that he would make Jesus a king over as much land as He wanted if He would just give in to the temptation and worship him. But Jesus said no to the Devil every time. He would not give in to the temptation because He was faithful to His father in heaven.

The next time you see an empty bottle or can and it is just lying on the ground as some more litter, I hope that you will think of the temptation that someone had and gave in to it. Then you will also think about the time that Jesus was tempted and did not give in. God wants us to be faithful and to resist temptation to do wrong.

Thank you very much for listening and helping me, and remember that God loves you always. Amen.

Let's Go Fishing

Matthew 4:12-23

Jesus called out, "Come along with me and I will show you how to fish for the souls of men!" (v. 19)

Object: *A member of your congregation who is a good fisherman and can tell the children a few things a good fisherman must know to catch fish.*

Good morning, boys and girls. Today we have a very special guest who is going to tell us some things that many people spend a whole lifetime trying to learn and never really do. How many of you like to go fishing? (Let them answer.) Almost all of you. Did you know that some people are good fishermen, and some people are not? I am not a good fisherman, but I have invited a good friend of ours to tell you and me how to catch fish the next time we go fishing. (Introduce the man and ask him some questions about fishing and about his equipment.)

Wasn't that interesting? Now you know why Mr. ..... is a good fisherman. He knows the little tricks that a fisherman has to know. That is what Jesus was trying to tell his disciples when he told them that if they followed him, he would teach them how to catch men for God's kingdom. He told them that he would make them fishers for men. We know that you can't just walk down the street and say, "Follow Jesus" and have people decide to follow him. We know that you can't just march around with signs, or hand out books to make people disciples of Jesus. If we want people to know about him and his Heavenly Father, then we have to know all we can about Jesus. We must also live the way that Jesus wants us to live and share our love with other people.

This is what Jesus meant when he told the disciples that he would make them fishers of men. He taught them how a Christian lives, thinks, acts and loves. We want to know as much about Jesus and maybe even more than our friend knows about catching fish. That is why it is important that you learn about him in Sunday school and worship in church. That is why you should share your life at home with your friends. That is why you must forgive others and ask their forgiveness when you do something wrong.

Being a Christian is learning, learning, and more learning. If you want to be a good fisherman, then you ask a man who knows how to catch fish. If you want to learn about being a Christian, you learn from Jesus and from disciples who have learned from him.

The next time you see someone doing a good job of fishing, I want you to watch him carefully. The next time you think about being a Christian, I want you to watch another one closely and learn all that you can about the way he lives with Jesus.

God bless you. Amen.

Solid As a Rock

Matthew 7:21-29

"So then, everyone who hears these words of mine and obeys them will be like a wise man who built his house on the rock . . . But everyone who hears these words of mine and does not obey them will be like a foolish man who built his house on the sand." (vv. 24, 25)

Objects: A big rock, some sand, a wash tub, and a bucket of water.

Good morning, boys and girls. Today I want to tell you about one of the favorite stories of Jesus, and how he used it to convince people of the truth. Jesus was not just any old storyteller. He was the best. One day he told people that there were two kinds of listeners. One kind of listener was like a man who built his house on a rock. Not many of us have ever built a house, but I can show you what he meant.

Suppose that you were building a house, and you wanted it to be strong and last for years. You want a good house to last a long time, and one of the most important choices that you must make is to build it in the right place. If you build your house on a rock it may be hard to dig a basement, but it will not slide away or break down. That's what Jesus said, and I am going to prove it. First, I will try to break the rock with my fist. (Give the rock a hard slap.) It didn't crack or fall away. Next, I will pretend that I am a big wind. (Blow across the rock.) Nothing happened again. Perhaps I should try a little water pretending that I am a flood and see what happens to the rock. Still nothing. This looks like a good place to build a house. But what if I do the same things to this sand? Do you know what will happen? (Let them answer.) Let's try it. (Slap it, blow on it and pour the water over it.) Disaster. Any house would not have much of a chance if it was built on the sand.

Jesus used this kind of a story to show the difference between people who listened to what he said and obeyed him, and those who listened and did not obey him. The people who listened and obeyed were like people who built their houses on a rock. The ones who did not obey were like the ones who built their houses on the sand. It makes a difference.

I know a lot of people who are like the ones who build on a sand pile. It seems a lot easier to work in sand than it does in rock. But it doesn't last. That's the same way it is with obeying Jesus. Sometimes it seems like Jesus is expecting too much of us. It seems hard and it would be a lot easier to do it the other way. But if we want things to be right, and we want to have good lives, we must trust in Jesus and do what he says.

The next time you see a rock or some sand, you can think about the time Jesus told about the difference between people who built their houses to last, or the ones who were looking for an easy way that failed. Amen.

Jesus Makes Us Well

Matthew 9:9-13

Jesus heard them and answered, "People who are well do not need a doctor, but only those who are sick." (v. 12)

Object: A doctor's white coat or stethoscope.

Good morning, boys and girls. How are you today? Do you feel well or are you slightly dizzy? Is there anyone here with a headache, stomach ache, bad cough, or broken bones? (Let them answer.) If any of you feel bad at all let me know and I will take care of you immediately. (Put on your white coat.) You know who I think I am, don't you? That's right, a doctor. Do you think that I would make a good doctor? (Let them answer.) You don't. When do you go to a doctor? (Let them answer.) That's right, when you are sick you go to a doctor. Do you ever go to a doctor when you are well? I don't think so. Most people go to the doctor when they are sick, or when they need to know something about their health.

People who are well don't need a doctor. At least that is what Jesus said, and he had a pretty good idea of what people should do, and when they should do it. Jesus was not interested in being a doctor, but instead he was trying to tell the people something else. He said when you are sick, you go to a doctor. He could have said that when you want to learn something you go to a teacher, or when you want to build a house, you go to a carpenter. Jesus was trying to tell us that you should go to the people who can give you help when you need help. If we have sinned, then we should go to the person who can help us with our sin. That means that we need a Savior, someone to forgive us. There is only one Savior, and only one who can forgive us for our sins. You know who that is. That's right, Jesus Christ.

That is what Jesus was trying to tell the people. We need a Savior, and we should look for the Savior. Without him we live in sin. With him we can be forgiven, and live with God. It's that simple, according to Jesus. Go to the place and the person where you can get the kind of help you need. All of us have sinned. Every one of us needs Jesus, but not all of us go to him. Some of us think that we can get rid of our sin by ourselves just as some of us think we can do without doctors, carpenters, and teachers. The only person who is hurt, is the person who doesn't go to the right place.

The next time you see your doctor you will think about the way he makes you well. Then you will also think about how Jesus is the Savior, and forgives us of our sin. Amen.

It Takes a Lot of Helpers

Matthew 9:35-10:7

Pray to the owner of the harvest that he will send out workers to gather in his harvest. (v. 38)

Objects: *A huge stack of dishes and a lot of towels.*

Good morning, boys and girls. How are you today? I want to share some thoughts with you today about working for Jesus. How many of you ever thought that Jesus wanted you to be one of his workers? (Let them answer.) Well, he does. As a matter of fact, he wants every one of you to work for him in some way. It takes a lot of people to tell everyone in the world about the love that God wants to share with us. Some people think that the work of God should be done by pastors and Sunday school teachers. But it can't be done that way.

Let's suppose that there was a job, a big job, and you were in charge of it. Let's say that you had to wash, dry, and put away all of these dishes before you could go out and play. How long do you think that it would take to get this job done? (Let them answer.) That's right, a long time. Do you think that you would ever get outside to play ball, tag, or jump rope? I don't think so. But now, suppose you could get as many people as I have towels to help you do the dishes? Now how long do you think it would take? That's right, not very long at all. The dishes would be done so fast that you would think that the big job was really a pretty small one.

That is the way Jeus would like to have it happen in this

world. He wishes that people would come to God and ask him for a job so that the work could be done. It would not only get done, but everyone would have a good time doing it. Jesus needs help to tell the story about how God really loves all of the people and wants to share the good things in this world with them.

But it takes all of us. If only a few help, it is going to take a long time. It will seem like the job will never be done and many people may never hear about it while they live here on earth. That would be a shame. But if you tell someone about the great things that Jesus did for all of us and they listen to what you say and share it with someone else, then soon everyone will know.

The next time you have a job, and someone helps you do it, I want you to think about the time I asked you to share with me the job of telling all of the world about Jesus and God's love. If you remember, then my job will be easier and many more people will hear the things we want the whole world to know about God. Amen.

He's Counted Every One of Them

Matthew 10:26-33

As for you, even the hairs of your head have all been counted. (v. 30)

Object: *Hair. (Perhaps you can collect several samples from a number of people.)*

Good morning, boys and girls. I brought with me this morning something that all of you have. Some of you have a lot of it. (Show them the hair samples.) What do we call this? That's right, hair. All of us have hair and while some of us have more than others, we all know what we mean when we speak of hair. Some of us like to comb it and shape it in different ways, and others of us like to brush it as quickly as possible and forget it. There are different colors of hair and we know people by the color of hair they have. Some of us have blonde hair, while others have black, brown, red, or orange. I don't think that anyone here has gray hair but there are some of us who have gray hair when we get a little older. I often hear people talk about the red-headed girl or the black-haired boy. That is one way we know people.

All of us know that God watches over us. We have heard that all of our lives. As a matter of fact, some people think that God knows us too well. I don't know about that, but I do know that the Bible teaches us that God cares about us so much that he actually knows the number of hairs we have on our heads. Can you imagine that kind of caring? How many hairs do you have on your head? (Take a quick guess from each child.) If I gave you a chance to sit here and count the hairs I have in my hand it would take you almost all morning. There are a lot of hairs in a small clump like this. Yet the Bible tells us that God cares so much for us that he even knows how many hairs are growing on each of our heads.

I think that is wonderful. God cares so much about me that he even has that kind of information. If he knows how many hairs, then think of the other things he knows about us. He knows about our sadness and our happiness. He knows how we feel about others and how they feel about us. He knows when we have done wrong, and when we have done right. Most of all he knows how we feel about him.

God cares. I know it, and now you know it. The next time you brush your hair, or have it cut, I want you to think about God caring for you so much that he would even know the number of hairs that you have on your head. Amen.

Nothing To Worry About

Matthew 11:25-30

Come to me and I will give you rest — all of you who work so hard beneath a heavy yoke. (v. 28)

Object: *A hard hat.*

Good morning, boys and girls, and how are you today? How many of you are hard workers? (Let them answer.) Very good. I like hard workers who like hard work. I brought with me this morning a hat, but it is not just any hat. Do you know what we call this kind of a hat? (Let them answer.) That's right, a hard hat. Do you know why we call it a hard hat? Very good, Because it is made of hard plastic or hard metal. It protects the person who wears it from anything that might fall on his head. Have you ever seen men building a house and wearing one of these hats? It makes them feel safe to have one of them on. While someone is working up above, the man down below does not have to worry about something, like a hammer, being dropped on his head and possibly killing him. The hard hat protects him from almost any kind of danger. Before they made these hats, a lot of people were hurt while they were working and a lot more people worried all of the time they worked that something might happen to them.

People worry a lot. Worry makes you tired, just like hard work makes you tired. When a person is tired, he is not the same as when he is fresh. Do you know how grouchy you get when you are tired? (Let them answer.) It is an awful feeling, isn't it? Men who wear these hats work better, worry less, and so they are not as tired as they might be without them. Jesus knew about hard work, worry, and being tired. He knew that men and women, boys and girls, were not their best when they felt like that. Some people grow old in a hurry and Jesus knew it. He wanted people to stop worrying and growing old while they lived on God's good earth, so he told them that if they would trust him, he would help. People worry about their sins against God and their sins against their friends. It makes them grouchy and very unhappy. Jesus said to tell him about their problems, and he would forgive them for what they did wrong, and give them strength to do what is right.

Trusting Jesus is like wearing a hard hat. When you have Jesus, you can stop worrying and live the way God wants you to. That is the best way to be. The next time you see someone wearing a hard hat, I want you to think about being a friend with Jesus and trusting him to make your life better. Amen.

Let It Grow!

Matthew 13:1-9

But some fell on good soil, and produced a crop that was thirty, sixty, and even a hundred times as much as he had planted. (v. 8)

Object: *Some good-looking soil.*

Good morning, boys and girls. Today I have brought something which I know all of you have seen, played in, and even carried around on your skin for part of the day. How many of you know what this is? (Show them the soil.) That's right, dirt or ground. Another word for it is soil. What good is dirt or soil? (Let them answer.) Very good. You can grow things in it. How many of you have ever grown something in the soil? (Let them answer.) A lot of you have done it. I think this is wonderful and I am pleased because you are going to be a big help today. Some of you have grown flowers, grass, and trees in the soil. Some of you have grown vegetables. Have any of you ever planted a seed and waited for it to grow and nothing happened? (Let them answer.) Some of you have had that happen, too, haven't you. The soil makes a lot of difference since you can grow some things in some soil but you cannot grow anything in other soil. The soil makes a big difference.

The same thing is true with people. God said that he has the same good news for everyone. He doesn't tell one person one thing and another person another. He tells all of us about his love and what he wants to share with us, but it helps some people and others it doesn't seem to help at all. I think you know what I mean. Jesus died for everyone, but some people pay no attention to Jesus and don't seem to care if he died at all. God made the sun to shine and the rain to fall, but some people think that it happens all by itself and that God had nothing to do with it. Some people love God and share everything they have with anyone who needs it, but other people hate God, and are very selfish. That means there are good people and bad people, but it does not mean that there is a good God and a bad God. God is the same. He loves us all the same but the people are different because they allow God to love them differently.

God says that when we allow him to love us, we will grow in the best way a boy, girl, man, or woman can grow. That is, if we are like the good dirt or soil. But if we are like the bad soil, it doesn't make any difference how much God loves us, we will not grow anything in us that is good.

It makes a difference how we are to God, just like it makes a big difference how the soil is for plants. God loves us, and wants us to grow in the good ways, but it is important that we are ready for God's love. Amen.

Don't Pull Them Out

Matthew 13:24-30

Let them both grow together until the harvest and I will tell the reapers to sort out the thistles and burn them and put the wheat in the barn. (v. 30)

Object: *Some weeds (thistles if possible.)*

Good morning, boys and girls. How many of you help in the yard? Do any of you cut the grass, rake up the trimmings, or plant the flowers? (Let them answer.) Do any of you ever pull weeds? (Let them answer.) That is a tough job. It seems like it will never end. I think the part about pulling weeds I don't like the most is that I always pull up some of the grass with the weeds. Either that or I pull the weed and the root stays in the ground and it soon grows another weed on top. Do any of you ever do that? (Let them answer.) Suppose that you were a farmer and you had weeds in your field of wheat. What would you do with the weeds that were mixed up in the wheat? (Let them answer.) If you pulled them, you would also pull the wheat and it would not be ready to be picked. You can't burn the weeds and, if you use weed killer, you might also poison the wheat. What do you think you would do?

Jesus had a problem like this, only the problem was about people rather than wheat and weeds. People were always asking why the bad people were allowed to live and get rich along with the good people. Have you ever heard a question like that? If you look at a weed, you see that it almost always grows faster and gets bigger than the wheat in the field or the grass in your yard. People wanted to know why God allowed the bad people to have everything that the good people had and sometimes even more. The people thought that if they were God, they would take the bad people away.

Jesus had an answer and it is a good one. If you are a good farmer and you have weeds growing in your wheat, you let them grow until the time to gather them up. The weeds and the wheat grow together. But when the wheat is picked, it is kept to be made into bread, but the weeds are taken away and burned.

Jesus says that God does about the same thing. God lets the bad people live with the good people here on earth. But when the time comes for us to live with God in heaven, then God will choose the ones who have been good and he keeps them. The bad ones are kept out of heaven.

The next time you see a weed and you wonder why it has so much room, I want you to think about the way that God takes care of people. It may seem like the weed gets the best of it, but it is only for a little while. When the right time is near, God takes care of the ones who love and obey him and keeps them away from the ones who have been bad and hateful. Love God and ask for his forgiveness when you have done wrong and you will never be treated like a weed. Amen.

Something Old and Something New

Matthew 13:44-52

So he replied, "This means, then, that every teacher of the law who becomes a disciple in the Kingdom of Heaven is like a homeowner who takes new and old things out of his storage room." (v. 52)

Object: *A big box with things to sort before moving.*

Good morning, boys and girls. How many of you have ever moved from one house to another? (Let them answer.) That is a big job, isn't it? Did you help your mom and dad get ready for the move? (Let them answer.) It is kind of exciting, but it is also hard work. One of the hardest jobs in moving your home is making the decisions about what to take with you, what to give away or sell, and what to throw away. Maybe you will remember when you had to go through your toys and books and decide what you wanted to take with you.

I brought a box of things along with me this morning that I must decide on if I am going to move. (Begin to go through the box and sort the things that you want to keep and the things that you do not want. Give your reasons for doing so.) It isn't easy. Some things are only good because I remember happy things when I hold them. Other things are very important and I could not do without them.

The reason I have told you this is because people have the same kind of problems when they read the Bible. The Bible is the story of how God made his world and worked with the people in the world. As the people grew and learned things from God, he taught them new things. Some of the things he taught them first were only happy memories and did not have any use anymore. Other things were very important and should never be forgotten. When Jesus lived on earth, he taught the people lots of new things about God that they did not know before. The things Jesus taught were so important that people had to give up the old ways and do things the way God wanted them to do it now. Other things, Jesus said, were good memories, but there was a better way to do it. Jesus said that disciples should know the way God taught the people to grow, but that they should now do things the way he taught them. We must do it that way today. We read the Old and the New Testament and where Jesus changes something that was in the Old Testament, we must change, too.

It is like moving from the old house to the new. When you go to the new house, you are living there, so even when you remember how you used to do things, you must now do different things in the new house. We are Christians and we live the way Jesus teaches us to live today. Learning about God is like moving. There will always be new things to learn and better ways to live if we follow the teachings of God and love the way he teaches us. Amen.

The 5,000-Person Picnic

Matthew 14:13-21

"What!" they exclaimed, "We have exactly five small loaves of bread and two fish!" (v. 17)

Objects: A jar of peanut butter and some bread.

Good morning, boys and girls. I want you to pretend with me today that we are going on a picnic and that we are going to take with us some peanut butter and bread. How many of you like peanut butter? (Let them answer.) That's good, because that is all I have for a picnic. Do you think that one jar will be enough for all of us? (Let them answer.) I think so, too. We have a loaf of bread and a jar of peanut butter, and we are going to have a wonderful time.

But suppose that after we get to where we are going we find a lot of new friends and we meet some old ones that we haven't seen for a long time? It would sure make for a fun time, wouldn't it? (Let them answer.) Can you imagine the ball games, the swings, the frisbees flying through the air, and all of the other things that would go on at a great picnic like this one? There would be children everywhere. Hundreds, and maybe even thousands, of children playing in the park and having a wonderful time. But, then it would be time to eat and none of the children brought anything with them. What would they all eat? What do you think you would do? (Let them answer.) You are right, we have a jar of peanut butter; but that was for us. There is not enough peanut butter for everyone. What do you think we should do? (Let them answer.) It would really be a problem, wouldn't it?

It was this kind of thing that happened to Jesus one day. He went with his disciples to the far side of a lake where they thought they would be alone. The problem was that everyone loved Jesus so much that they followed him wherever he went. After a while everyone became hungry, but no one had thought to bring any food with them. Well, one person remembered, but he only had a few fish and some bread. It could not feed the five thousand men — and who knows how many more women and children — who had come to hear and love Jesus. Some of the disciples told Jesus to send the people home. But Jesus knew that the people had come too far and that they would faint from hunger before they got back home. Then Jesus did a wonderful thing that only he could do. He said a prayer over the few fish and told the disciples to take the fish and give them away to everyone who wanted some, until they ran out. Do you know what happened? They never ran out. It was a miracle. Five thousand people were fed all of the fish and bread they wanted and there was some left over. It was some picnic!

We can't do that with our peanut butter. We don't have the power that Jesus has, but we will never forget how Jesus fed 5,000 people. The next time you sit down to eat a peanut butter sandwich, I hope you will think about the day Jesus had a picnic and fed everyone with a few fish and a couple of loaves of bread. Amen.

Safe With Jesus

Matthew 14:22-23

But Jesus immediately spoke to them, "Don't be afraid!" he said. (v. 27)

Objects: *A big stick, a flashlight, or the hand of a friend.*

Good morning, boys and girls. Do you remember the last time you were afraid or scared? (Let them answer.) Do you remember what caused it? (Let them answer.) None of us likes to be frightened. It is an awful feeling and we would do almost anything to keep it from happening again. I remember some times when I was afraid and I wished I had something that would help me get over that scary feeling I had in my stomach. Once I was frightened by a big dog that barked and barked and looked like he was going to bite my leg off. I wished I had a big stick to keep the dog away from me. (Show the stick.) I also remember the times when I had to feel around in the dark, and I don't like to be in the dark for very long. (Flash the light.) I wished that I had a big flashlight to turn on so that I could see better. I also remember the times that I was afraid because I felt sick and I wished that there were someone to hold my hand. That would have helped a lot.

We are not the only people who were ever afraid. It happens to everyone. I remember a story in the Bible where Peter, the big fisherman, was very frightened. The disciples were in their boat crossing the lake when tne waves got very high and the boat began to rock as if it were going to tip over. The sky was dark, the waves were high, and they thought they were going to drown. If you are afraid in a dark room, imagine how they felt on a dark lake with water splashing them in the face and the boat going up and down and back and forth. They were frightened. But, if that weren't enough, they looked up in the dark and saw a man walking on the water. He wasn't swimming, he wasn't in another boat, but he was walking on the water! Now they were really frightened and they began to cry and yell as loud as they could.

That's when Jesus, who was the man walking on the water, spoke to them in a calm voice, "Don't be afraid." Just hearing his voice made them all feel better. He was like a big stick or a flashlight or the hand of a friend. Jesus made them all feel much better simply by being there. You don't have to wait for a storm or a scary experience to let Jesus make you feel safe and good. Jesus is always like that for everybody who needs him. If you want him to, he will be with you today. He will help you in any trouble and share his joy with you when everything is right. The next time you are afraid, ask Jesus to share himself with you and see how much better you feel. Amen.

The Bigger the Better

Matthew 15:21-28

"Woman," Jesus told her, "your faith is large and your request is granted." And her daughter was healed right then. (v. 28)

Objects: *Cereal boxes in different sizes, such as regular, snack, large, and giant.*

Good morning, boys and girls. How many of you like cereal for breakfast in the morning? Oh, good, a lot of you like cereal. I am always so surprised when I look in the kitchen cupboard and see all of the different boxes of cereal that we keep for breakfast. Not only are there a lot of different kinds, but there are all different sizes of boxes. Take a look at what I brought with me. Here is the smallest one I could find. It is called the snack size. But there are others. The regular size is pretty big, but it is nothing compared to the large size, and that is even small when you compare it to the giant size. We have all kinds of sizes of cereal boxes, and I know that if I gave you a choice of the box you wanted, you would take the largest one I have. We like things that are big. The bigger the better.

I think the same thing is true of our faith. The bigger our faith, the better. That's what Jesus said. He knew that the bigger our faith was, the more we could do with our faith. For instance, there was a woman who had a sick daughter and wanted her healed. She was not of the regular followers, but she believed that Jesus had great power. She asked Jesus several times if he would help her daughter. Jesus did not jump right up and do what she asked, but instead he asked her why she wanted him to do it and why she did not ask someone else? The woman told Jesus each time that she believed in him. Finally, after a lot of time and questioning, Jesus did what she asked, but he told her that he did what she wanted because she had a great faith. She believed that Jesus had great power and that no one else could do for her what he could.

That is what faith is all about. You can believe in a lot of people and a lot of people can help you. But people can only do a little bit, when you compare it to what Jesus can do for you. Having faith in people is like the snack size or the regular size. But, if you have faith, great faith in God, it is like having the giant size box. It is so much greater, but it also gives you so much more.

The woman who asked Jesus to heal her daughter had a great faith, and Jesus told her so. Each of us wants to work on his own faith so that we can grow and expect the really big things to happen to us, just as they happened to the woman in our story.

The next time you see a cereal box, I hope you look at the size of it and then you can think about the size of your faith. If you believe with all of your heart that Jesus is your Savior, then you know what size your faith is. A big faith brings big results. Amen.

The Most Important Thing

Matthew 16:21-26

Then Jesus said to his disciples, "If anyone wants to be a follower of mine, let him deny himself and take up his cross and follow me." (v. 24)

Object: *Some kind of shirt or hat showing that you belong to a team.*

Good morning, boys and girls. How many of you have ever been on a team of any kind? (Let them answer.) It may be a team at school or on the playground or anywhere that there would be teams. Good. Some of you have been on a team. Did you wear anything special such as a hat, shirt, or pin to identify your team? I have a hat that shows that I am a member of a team. My team is the Cincinnati Reds. The Reds is a special team that plays baseball. If you want to be a member of that team, you have to give up everything else and just play baseball. You can't work in a shoe factory or teach school and still be a member of the team. Every day for seven or eight months you must practice baseball and play baseball games. You have to give up almost everything else to be a member of the Cincinnati Reds team. That means a lot. In order to be a member of the Reds' team, you have to work really hard, just like you would if you had any other job.

The same thing is true about being a follower of Jesus. To belong to the team that Jesus is putting together is not easy. Jesus knew it. He told everybody, if they were going to believe in him as the Lord, they could not believe in anyone else. You have to give up all other kinds of gods to believe in Jesus. Sometimes you have to put Jesus ahead of some things that you like pretty well, but are things that get in the way of Jesus. Jesus is first. Jesus is so important that nothing else is as important.

We are Christians, and we belong to the team that Jesus is making for heaven. We must be ready to put Jesus first and everything else second. It is the only way we can belong to the team that Jesus is getting ready. Jesus knew that not everyone wanted to be on his team, but he can't change the rules. You must be ready to put Jesus first and everything else second.

Everyone is invited to be a Christian. The Cincinnati Reds are invited to be Christians and many of them are. When it comes to baseball playing and being a follower of Jesus, they choose Jesus. Baseball is second for them. Being a follower of Jesus is first. If something came up and the ballplayer had to make a choice, then he would choose Jesus. You will have to make the same kind of choices. Some days you will think that you would rather do something that Jesus would not want you to do. You have to choose and put Jesus first or second. When you make that choice, you will know if you are on the team with Jesus or not. I know that you will choose Jesus, because his is the best team in the world. Amen.

What a Great Experience!

Matthew 17:1-9

Peter blurted out, "Sir, it's wonderful that we can be here! If you want me to, I'll make three shelters, one for you and one for Moses and one for Elijah." (v. 4)

Objects: *Some camping equipment.*

Good morning, boys and girls. Have you ever traveled in a state park or some other beautiful place and wished that you lived there? I have. Some places look like heaven itself. Wherever you look you see beautiful things like lakes, trees, green grass, birds and animals. Everything seems just perfect. When I am traveling and I see something like that I want to stop and get out my camping equipment and just sit down and enjoy all of the things around me. I feel that I never want to leave. This is the place for me! (Take out your camping equipment and begin to set it up as though you were making camp.) How many of you know what I mean? (Let them answer.)

There was a time like that for Peter, James, and John. They were with Jesus on the top of a mountain. It was a wonderful time to be with Jesus, and then things began to happen that made it even more beautiful. Right before their eyes Jesus seemed to change into a brilliant light. His face and hands were like the sun, and his clothes were the most beautiful that they had ever seen. And to top it all off, there were Moses, the lawgiver, and Elijah, the prophet, standing right beside Jesus. They had been dead for hundreds of years, but they were alive and standing by Jesus. It was the most wonderful experience of their lives, and Peter wanted it to stay that way. He even suggested to Jesus that he build some tents so that Jesus and Moses and Elijah would have a place to stay. He didn't think about building a tent or shelter for himself or for James and John. They didn't need one. All they wanted to do was watch and listen. It was marvelous. But it didn't last because Jesus knew that they could not live on the mountain. There were things to do and people to help.

That is the same for us. You can't live the rest of your life in a park. No matter how beautiful it is, you must go back home sooner or later. Children must go to school and parents must work.

That day in the life of Jesus was called the Day of the Transfiguration. It was a very special day. But Jesus came down from the mountain and went back to work with the people. He loved the day he spent on the mountain with his father in heaven and with Moses and Elijah, but he did not stay there. That's something for us to remember when we think that we only want to live and stay in the beautiful places. We, too, must go back to work with the people who need us so we can help them to know God better.

Thank you very much for sharing with me this morning, and remember that God loves you always. Amen.

How To Be a Leader

Matthew 20:17-28

Anyone wanting to be a leader among you must be your servant. (v. 25b)

Objects: *A trash bag filled with paper; a dish towel; a can of furniture polish.*

Good morning, boys and girls. How many of you would like to be a leader? Lots of you like to be leaders. Why would you want to be a leader? (Let them answer.) Those are all good reasons. How does someone get to be a leader? (Let them answer.) Leaders are chosen, aren't they? But why is one person chosen to be a leader and another one is not? (Let them answer.) That is really a hard question. Some people just seem to be leaders all of the time, and other people never seem to be chosen. Let me see if I can be of some help.

A long time ago the mother of John and James, who were disciples of Jesus, asked Jesus if he would name her sons as leaders and give them a special place in the new world that he was building. I can't think of a better place to be a leader than in God's world. But Jesus wanted to know if John and James' mother knew what she was asking. Being a leader is never easy, and it would be especially hard in something that Jesus was building. Of course, the disciples wanted to know how all of them could be leaders with Jesus, so he told them that anyone who wanted to lead must do something else first. Do you know what that was? (Let them answer.) Jesus said that they must first be servants before they could be chosen to lead. Do you know what a servant does? (Let them answer.) That's right, a servant is someone who helps others.

I want to show you an example of what I mean. Suppose I told you to take the trash bag and fill it with trash. Then suppose I told you to take this towel and wash the dishes, and then the cleaner and polish the furniture. If I told you to do that and made sure that you did it, you would be a servant but not a leader. Everyone else would be glad that I had not picked on them. But suppose you took the trash bag, towel, and cleaner and went to work on your own to clean up the place. I think you would still be a servant, but you would also be a leader. Others would be impressed by your wonderful attitude, and they might even volunteer to help. Then you would become a leader since they would be following your good example.

That is what Jesus meant when he said that people would have to be servants before they could lead. You don't start leading until you first are serving. I think that is a good lesson to learn. I hope that you remember it and also that God loves you always.

God bless you. Amen.

Time for a Parade

Matthew 21:1-11

*And some in the crowd threw down their coats along the road
ahead of him, and others cut branches from the trees and spread
them out before him. (v. 8)*

Object: *Palms.*

Good morning, boys and girls. Isn't this a marvelous day?
I love great festivals like Palm Sunday. You know what Palm
Sunday is all about, don't you? (Let them answer.) That's right,
it is the day that the people treated Jesus like a king when
He rode into Jerusalem on a donkey and rode through the
city. It had been a couple of very hard years for Jesus. He
loved what he did, and he was glad that so many people were
interested in learning more about God and how much he loved
them. He could count hundreds of people whom he had healed from sickness and from being crippled. But there were a
lot of people who did not believe him and they made it hard,
very hard, for him to teach or heal. Some people called him
a devil and others hated him because people they thought
should follow them were instead following Jesus. Jesus did
not just teach religion. He lived it. The times were hard and
the disciples warned Jesus that if he went back to Jerusalem
He would be killed. It was a real danger, and Jesus knew it.
But he was the Messiah, and it was important that the people believe in him and what he taught.

Jesus was not much for parades or marches. He liked to
work and teach quietly. Most of the time He taught in the

church or temple or beside a lake or maybe even on the side of a hill. Many times he would just talk to people as he walked down the road. If he heard someone cry for help, he would stop and find the person who needed him and do what he could to help.

But this was a special day. The disciples had warned Jesus but he knew even better than they did how close he was to death. Still he wanted the people to know that God was the real king and the men who called themselves kings were not the real king. Jesus borrowed a donkey and began to ride very slowly into the great city of Jerusalem. When the people saw him coming and remembered all that he taught, they started to walk beside him and shout words that meant victory. Before long the crowds grew larger and larger. While nothing was planned, it turned into a great celebration. People took off their coats and threw them over the stones in the street so that it looked like a carpet to ride on. Then there were the shouts of "Hosanna, Hosanna, Hosanna" which means, "Save us, we pray." And then finally the people cut branches from the palm trees and waved them as they sang. It must have looked like a great green sea with rolling waves.

It was a great day for the people and for God, too. The people knew who really was the King. You can remember the day also when you raise your palm branch and call Jesus Christ the King.

God bless you. Amen.

Making Wrong Things Right

Matthew 21:28-32

"For John the Baptist told you to repent and turn to God and you wouldn't, while very evil men and prostitutes did. And even when you saw this happening, you refused to repent, and so you couldn't believe." (v. 32)

Objects: *Blackboard, chalk, and eraser.*

Good morning, boys and girls. How many of you have ever made a mistake? Good, almost everyone here has made a mistake and they know it. That is very important. It is easy to make mistakes, but it is hard to know it. I will tell you something even harder than knowing mistakes, and that is correcting them. How many of you know of some mistake that you made that you corrected and made right? (Let them answer.) It is hard to think of a mistake that you made right, isn't it?

I brought along something that I know all of you have used at one time or another. (Take out the board, chalk, and eraser.) All of us know that this is a chalk board and piece of chalk. What is the other thing that I have in my hand? (Let them answer.) That's right, it is an eraser. If I spell cat *kat* and someone tells me that I have made a mistake, I can erase the *k,* but then what have I to do? That's right, I have to put a *c* where the *k* was when I spelled it wrong. We all make mistakes and many of us know what the mistake is, but a lot of us never correct the mistake.

Jesus told some people about this when he was talking

about John the Baptist. John the Baptist had told a lot of people about their sins. He told them what they had done wrong and he told them how to make it right. Some did and others did not. Jesus was very upset with some of the people who thought that they were pretty good, but who were really worse than the people that everyone knew were bad. Jesus said some of the bad people who did things that everyone knew were wrong, listened to John and not only admitted that they were bad, but they did something about it. They changed their ways and lived good lives. Some of the people who hid their wrong things never said they did anything wrong and never changed because they were afraid that other people might find out about them. Jesus said that they were much worse than the people who did such bad things that everyone knew about. It is better, Jesus said, to say that you were wrong and start over than to hide your wrong and never do anything about it. That is what Jesus taught and what all of us have to learn. Perhaps you have done something that you wish you had not done. Don't worry about what other people will think. Tell God you are sorry and start over and you will feel wonderful. The people who listened to John the Baptist tell them of their mistakes and corrected them found out how right Jesus was and they were glad that they made things right.

Just Like Cinderella

Matthew 21:33-43

Then Jesus asked them, "Didn't you ever read in the Scriptures: 'The stone rejected by the builders had been made the honored cornerstone; how remarkable! what an amazing thing the Lord has done?' " (v. 42)

Object: *Slipper (Cinderella's).*

Good morning, boys and girls. How many of you know the story of Cinderella? (Let them answer.) Would anyone like to tell me what the story of Cinderella is about? (Let someone tell you the story as briefly as possible.) It sure is a good story, isn't it? Just imagine how you would feel if you were Cinderella and the Prince came to fit the beautiful slipper on your foot? Wouldn't that be wonderful? It sure would.

I think the saddest part of the story is the way that all of Cinderella's family treated her. Her stepmother and her stepsisters were so mean to her. I suppose they even pretended that she was not part of their family. They hated her because she was good and kind and did not complain. They were selfish and mean and griped about everything. But the Prince showed them, and everyone, who was really the one person that was filled with love and joy.

The Bible teaches us another story, but this one is not make believe. It is true, and it is a little bit like Cinderella. God sent Jesus to earth as the Savior. Jesus was filled with love for everyone and he was kind and treated people with lots of care. He came to save the people of Israel. But the selfish people were afraid of him and so they lied and cheated and did everything mean that they could to Jesus with the hope that he would get discouraged and stop teaching people about God. But Jesus was not a quitter, and even though some of the people hated him, he still shared his love with them. Even some of his own family thought he was crazy for helping the sick and the poor.

But God knew what he was doing. Even if his own people hated him, it did not stop God from saving the world. Jesus was ready to be the Savior for more than just the Jews. Jesus was willing to share his love with all of the people in the whole world. Some people thought that Jesus was crazy. Some thought that he was foolish and stupid, but God knew Jesus as his son and made him a king. Jesus is the King of the World and the Savior of every man. People may try to shame Jesus, but God honored him with his love and grace. Amen.

"Y'All come!"

Matthew 22:1-10 (11-14)

" *'Now go out to the street corners and invite everyone you see.' " (v.9)*

Objects: A letter and a newspaper.

Good morning, boys and girls. How many of you have ever written a letter? (Let them show their hands.) A letter is a very personal thing. When you write a letter it is for only one person to read, or maybe just a couple of people. How many of you have ever read a newspaper? (Let them show their hands again.) Everyone has read a newspaper. As a matter of fact all of us probably read the same newspaper every day. That is what newspapers are for. A newspaper is for everyone, while a letter is only for one person, or just a few. It is important for you to know the difference, because it is important in learning something about Jesus.

For a long time people thought that each group had their own God. God was kind of like a letter. God was only for a few people. The Jews thought that their God was only for them and no one else. They even thought that someday God was going to visit the earth as a King and be their leader. They were partly right. God did visit the earth as a King. He was not the kind of King they thought he would be, but he was a King. God sent them messages like letters telling them what the King was going to be like, where he would be born, and even that he would be killed by people who thought that they were doing God a favor. Only the Jews really had this information since God spoke to them in letters.

Well, the King was born and lived like God said he would live. Some of the people loved the King, but many hated him and the ones who hated him finally killed him by hanging him on a cross. That was the end of the letters. Now God really went to work and started telling the world about his son and the death of his son in newspapers. Everyone found out about the King and his love. God sent messages that everyone could read just like you and I read the newspapers. Now it wasn't a letter to the Jews, but a newspaper for all the people in the world.

God has a great plan for all of us. All of us can read about it in the Bible and share it with each other in love. Maybe the next time you see a letter, you will think about how only a few once knew about the King Jesus, but now when you see a newspaper you can be glad that God shared his son the King with the whole world. Amen.

It Looks Good, But . . .

Matthew 22:15-21

But Jesus saw what they were after. "You hypocrites!" he exclaimed. "Who are you trying to fool with your trick questions?" (v.18)

Object: *A balloon with a hole in it. (Option is to have a balloon with a hole in it for each child.)*

Good morning, boys and girls. How many of you heard the story that I read from the Bible this morning where Jesus shouted at some men and called them hypocrites? (Let them answer.) Some of you were listening, but I wonder if anyone here knows what a hypocrite is? Does anyone know what the word hypocrite means? (Let them answer.) It's a big word, and it means that someone is pretending to be something that he is not. He isn't playing a game, but he really tries to make people think that he is good, very good, when really he is sneaky bad.

Let me try to show you what I mean. I brought along some balloons to give you this morning. How many of you like to play with a balloon? They are really fun, aren't they? I suppose that you know what a person is supposed to do with a balloon don't you? (Let them answer.) That's right, you must blow them up. I am going to give each one of you a balloon and I want you to blow them up as fast as you can. (Pass out the balloons and encourage them to blow them up until someone discovers the hole in his balloon.) Isn't that awful! It looks like a perfectly good balloon and a lot of fun, but with a hole in it, I know it won't work.

That's what Jesus was trying to tell the people. A lot of people want you to think that they are perfect and that they have nothing wrong with them. They don't need anyone, including God because they want everyone to know that they are perfect. But they are really like the balloons. They look good on the outside, but when you try to use them, they are full of holes. That is what a hypocrite is. It is a person who looks like a balloon that is perfectly good, but really they are full of sins just like the balloon is full of holes. Hypocrites are pretenders.

All of us have sins. All of us need God. But we don't try to kid anyone or trick anyone into believing that we don't have sins. We come to God everyday and pray that he will forgive our sins and make us real people. We do not want to be like hypocrites who pretend, but we want to be sinners who are forgiven by God and made real believers. Amen.

The Most Important Rule

Matthew 22:34-40 (41-46)

"Sir, which is the most important command in the law of Moses?" (v. 36)

Object: A calendar.

Good morning, boys and girls. I brought with me this morning a calendar. It has twelve months and 365 days. I want you to tell me which you think is the most important day in the year. (Let them answer.) Which day would you choose? Is the most important day your birthday, Christmas, the Fourth of July, Easter, New Year's Day? What day would you choose?

It isn't easy, is it? All of us have a different idea of which day is the most important. Some men asked Jesus which commandment of Moses was the most important commandment. They wanted Jesus to tell them that "You shall not kill" is the most important or that "You shall have no other gods before me" is the most important. They wanted Jesus to pick one of the ten so that they could argue with him that another one was more important, or as important as the one he chose. Jesus was smarter than that, and he knew what they were trying to do. He knew that they were trying to trick him, and make him look bad in front of the people that were listening. Do you know what Jesus did? He told them that if they loved God with all of their hearts and minds and strength, and if they loved their neighbor as much as they loved themselves, they would be keeping all of the Ten Commandments. All of the Commandments are important.

That is the way it is with the calendar. Every day is important. If you live each day like it is the most important day, then all of the days that you live will be important. If you love God with all of your heart, mind, and strength, and your neighbor as much as yourself, then you will keep all of the Ten Commandments. What a wonderful lesson Jesus taught us that day.

They couldn't trick Jesus, but they learned something so important that day that they didn't try to trick him again. And the people who heard Jesus were really impressed by the way he spoke, and by the way he knew God the Father so well.

The next time you look at the calendar and try to figure out which day is the most important, maybe you will remember the day that Jesus taught that loving God and man was the way to keep the Ten Commandments. Maybe you will also remember that every day that you live is the most important day of your life. Amen.

Glad To Be a Toothpick

Matthew 23:1-12

But those who think themselves great shall be disappointed and humbled; and those who humble themselves shall be exalted. (v. 12)

Objects: *A wood match and a toothpick.*

Good morning, boys and girls. How many of you have ever looked at a tree, a big tree and thought to yourself, "Boy, would that big tree make a lot of matches." (Let them answer.) Did you ever do that or think of something like I just said? I don't suppose that you think this way, and not very many people do. We like to think of the big things that a tree will make. A tree will give woods to build a house, a fence, a desk, or something that is big and beautiful. When we see big trees, we don't think of them making matches or toothpicks. Those kinds of things are just too small. They are made out of what is left over. No one tries to make a match or a toothpick. You make things that small when you have made all of the big things you can think of and you have a little bit left over so you chop it up into matches and toothpicks.

That is the way people are. People like to think of themselves as great and getting greater. Because of that, they never like to think of themselves as doing little things. People want to be rich, powerful, and loved by everyone. Because people are like that, they are often disappointed. Another way of saying this is that people only want to be big houses or long fences or beautiful desks. Not very many people want to be matches and toothpicks. That is why there are so many disappointed people. God says that the people who think a lot of themselves are going to be disappointed. Everyone cannot be a house or a long fence. Someone has to be a match and a toothpick.

God says that the people who think they will be satisfied to be a toothpick or match are going to be very satisfied, and not only that, but they are going to be used for greater things. Just think, a match is not only a piece of wood, but it can start a great fire, which makes great heat and can keep a whole city warm. One little match can do all of this and maybe even more.

Jesus tried to teach people to be humble and not proud. He told them that it was better to be a good match than it was to hope to be a big house. I hope the next time you see a great tree, you will think about how it might make some good matches and toothpicks, and not just a big house or a long fence. If you start thinking like that, then you will know what Jesus meant when he told people that they should not think so much of themselves that they forget about God. Be humble and not proud is the way the Christian should act and be. Amen.

Here He Comes, Ready Or Not

Matthew 25:1-13

But while they were gone, the bridegroom came, and those who were ready went in with him to the marriage feast, and the door was locked. (v. 10)

Object: *Raised hand in form of Scout pledge.*

Good morning, boys and girls. How many of you know what the word "prepare" means? (Let them answer.) That's right, it means to "get ready." A Scout has a motto that says, "Be Prepared." That means that a Scout should always be ready for anything that could happen. He or she is alert, sharp, always looking and listening so that he or she can be of help to anyone who needs him or her. Whenever a Scout goes to a meeting, he or she always repeats the motto, "Be prepared," so that he or she will never forget to be ready when he or she is needed.

Scouts are not the only people who should have that motto. A Christian should be prepared also. Jesus told a story about how some people were ready when a certain thing happened and how some people were not ready. The story was about some women who were supposed to help a man get ready for his marriage. They didn't know what time he would come but they were supposed to be ready. They waited all day and no one came, but when the night came, only half of them were prepared. The ones who were prepared were the women who brought lanterns to give light when it got dark. The ones who were not prepared had no light and when it got dark they had to go to buy oil for their lanterns. While they were away the man who was getting married came and took with him the women who were ready. When the other women returned with their lights, the door was locked and they could not get inside where the others were. Jesus told this story so that we would know how important it is to be prepared.

When Jesus comes back to earth we are not going to know the day or the hour. He will come at any time. We must be ready for him and our lives must be in good order. Some people think "that Jesus stuff" can wait until they get old. They don't have time for it now. But Jesus says that there may not be time later. Being prepared for Jesus is like being prepared for a parade or for school in the morning. It means that you must be ready now. You can't wait until it happens to get ready. If you wait until it happens you will be too late. It will be over.

So we need to get ready for Jesus now. We need to be prepared. The next time you see a Scout I want you to think about the way he or she is prepared and when you think of that, you will remember that you must also be prepared for Jesus when he comes back to earth to share his life with us. Amen.

What God Expects

Matthew 25:14-30

For the man who uses well what he is given shall be given more, and he shall have abundance. (v. 29)

Object: *A bushel of apples or some fruit.*

Good morning, boys and girls. Today we are going to learn something about what God expects of us. We expect a lot from God but did you ever think that he expected something from us? He does. God expects something from all of his world. Let me show you what I mean.

I brought this bushel of apples along to give you some idea of how God expects his world to grow. The apples look good and most of us like to eat them, but did you know that all of these apples came from the same tree? They did. Did you also know that the seeds of the apple are what God uses to grow new apple trees? If you know that, then you know that God not only gave us the apples to eat, but he puts the seeds in apples so that there would be more apple trees and with more of them there will be more apples to eat. If we did not plant some of the seeds, we would soon run out of apples.

The same thing is true of our money. If we took our money and only spent it on ourselves for things that we like to eat or wear, we would soon run out of money. Money is to be used so that some of it goes to do things that will make more money. Some people use their money to buy tools so that they can make things with the tools and sell what they make for more money. God understands that and he wants us to use our money wisely, just like he wants us to use our apples wisely.

And if that is true with apples and money, then it is true with our lives. A man has only one life, but God expects him to use it so that the best kind of things happen. If a man is really good with his life he can make his family happy, his friends happy, and himself happy. That is the way God wants us to use our lives.

Now there is a promise made by God that is really important and something that all of us should remember. God promises us that if we use the things he gives us, he will give us more and more until we have more than we need. But if we do not use what God gives us, then he will take the little bit that we have away, and give it to people who will use it. Do you understand what God means?

If we don't plant some of the apple seeds in the ground, soon we will be out of apples. If we don't buy tools or things to do our work with, we will not have enough money to feed or clothe us. God tells us that he made the world for us to use in the right way.

The next time that you see an apple or even a dollar, I want you to ask yourself, if you are going to use it the right way. If you do, there will be a lot more of both, but if you don't, you may be looking at the last apple or dollar that you will ever see. Amen.

Helping People to Help

Matthew 25:31-46

"And I, the King, will tell them, 'When you did it to these my brothers, you were doing it to me!" (v. 40)

Object: *The small hand or hour hand on a watch or clock.*

Good morning, boys and girls. How many of you have ever taken a good look at a clock or watch? Do you know something about the way that the hands work? (Let them answer.) The very fast moving hand and the longest hand on the clock is called the second hand. Watch how quickly it moves around the clock. The next biggest hand is called the minute hand and it does not move as fast, but it moves a lot faster than the small one. Let's remember where the second biggest hand is on the clock, and we will look again in a few minutes to see how far it has moved. The third hand is a real slowpoke. It hardly moves at all. We cannot even notice it moving. It takes a whole hour to move from one number to the other number. But the great thing is that as one of the hands moves, it makes the other hand move, and then when it moves, it makes the third one move. The biggest makes the second biggest move, and the second biggest makes the smallest move. Whatever happens to one makes it happen to the other.

The reason I have shown you this is because I hope that it will teach you and me something about how we work with Jesus. People have always wanted to do good things for God. They think if they are good to God, then God will be good to them. That sounds right, but Jesus said it didn't work exactly that way. He told people that when they did good things for his people, they were doing good things for God. Feed hungry people and you are doing something for God. Visit lonely people and you are visiting God. Help people who are sick and you are making God feel much better. People don't like to give their food to other people and they don't like to use their time to visit lonely people, but God says that is the way you do good things for God. They wish that they could do it for God and not for others. But Jesus told all of the people who really needed help. When you are doing that you are really doing good for God.

That is the way the clock works. When the biggest hand moves it moves the second biggest, and the second biggest moves the littlest. Pretend that you are the biggest hand and you do something for someone who is hungry or lonely. The hungry and the lonely are the second biggest hand. Now that you have made them move, they will make the littlest hand move to the next hour. God says that the way to his heart is when you and I help the people who need our help. It is a great way to learn how to love other people and the best way to show our love for God. Amen.

A Crown For The King

Matthew 28:16-20

He told his disciples, "I have been given all authority in heaven and earth." (v. 18)

Object: *A Crown.*

Good morning, boys and girls. How many of you have ever wanted to be a king? What do you think you would look like if you were a king? (Let them answer.) That sounds very good. You would look rich, wouldn't you? Would you wear something on your head that would make me think that you were a king? That's right, you would wear a crown. Kings wear crowns, don't they? Why do they do that? (Let them answer.) Those are pretty good reasons, but I want to share another one with you. A crown is a symbol of authority. Authority means to be in charge. A king has authority, and when he wears a crown he is showing everyone that he is in charge.

I don't have a crown, and you don't have a crown. We are not authorities. At least we are not the authority country, or any other country. Jesus is a king. He is the king of heaven and earth. He has authority over everything. God the Father gave Jesus that authority. There is no one else in heaven or earth in charge. That is the way God wanted it, and that is the way it is. When Jesus gives a command, it is with real authority. If we want to work with God, then we must live the way Jesus says we should.

The disciples knew this. They believed they received their

orders from Jesus like commands. If Jesus told them to go to a new nation and teach about the things Jesus taught, then they went to that nation. If Jesus commanded them to baptize the people in the new nation who believed, then they baptized them. The disciples moved, and taught, and loved wherever and whoever the Lord Jesus said they should.

A crown is the symbol of authority for earthly kings, but for the King of the world there is no crown made of gold or silver. Jesus does not get his power from the army or navy. Jesus gets his power from God the Father, and He uses it with love.

The next time you hear about a king, any king, and you think about his wearing a crown, I want you to think about the real King. I want you to think about Jesus and the power that he has to rule the whole world. Will you do that? Good. God bless you. Amen

Getting Ready

Mark 1:1-8

In the book written by the prophet Isaiah, God announced that he would send his Son to earth, and that a special messenger would arrive first to prepare the world for his coming. (v. 2)

Object: A garden rake.

Good morning, boys and girls. I brought with me this morning a tool that I am sure all of you have used before. It's a rake. Do you know how you use this kind of rake? (Let someone show you.) That's good. Where do you use it? (Let them answer.) That's right, in the garden. Do you dig with it or plant with it? Of course not. You use a rake to prepare the ground for the seeds and to make the ground smooth after you have put the seeds in the ground. Preparing something means to get it ready and making it smooth means that you take out the lumps so that it is all even.

John the Baptizer was a rake. That's what the Bible says. The Bible tells us that John the Baptizer was sent by God to prepare the way for Jesus. He was supposed to make things smooth so that people would listen and follow Jesus. John had to smooth out a lot of rough places. People were ugly and filled with sin. They didn't listen to anyone and the only person that each man thought about was himself. God knew how it was and so he had a plan. That plan was to send a man called John the Baptizer first, and for him to tell the people about their sin and all of their ugliness and hope that some people would listen and change a bit.

John raked a lot. He preached and taught thousands of people about the way things were bad and getting worse. He also told the people about a man whom God was sending called Jesus, who was the Son of God. If people would listen to Jesus, they would find out the wonderful secrets that only God knew and only God could share. People listened. Not all of the people listened, but some of them did. The ones who did not listen were the big lumps of dirt that never do get smooth. The rake just pulls them out and pushes them away. John did that with some and he made them angry at him. But John knew what he had to do and he did it. John wanted to make a path smooth so that some people who were ready would listen to Jesus, the Son of God. I guess you know what a good rake John the Baptizer was. He was the best rake that a man could be. People heard Jesus and they believed in God's plan.

Maybe the next time you see a rake, you will think of John the Baptizer, and when you do, I hope you think about what a hard job it was to do. John the Baptizer was called by God to prepare the world for Jesus and to make the bumpy way a lot smoother. Amen.

Being Faithful Followers

Mark 8:27-35

Then Jesus called the crowd and His disciples to Him. "If anyone wants to come with me," He told them, "he must forget himself, carry his cross, and follow me." (v.34)

Objects: *Some crosses made of whatever material that you would like and one large one that can be seen by everyone. The small crosses should be given out to each of the children.*

Good morning, boys and girls. Today I brought with me an object that I know all of you have seen and we have talked about many times. (Hold up the cross.) This is what? (Let them answer.) That's right, this is a cross. Why do we talk so much about a cross? (Let them answer again.) That's right, this is where Jesus died. He died on a cross. It was an ugly sight. If you or I would have seen it happen, we would have gotten sick to our stomach. No one would ever want to die like this because it was so painful and very disgraceful. But that is the way some men decided that Jesus should die so they could have things their way without Jesus reminding them that their way was wrong. This is the reason they killed Him.

That isn't the real reason Jesus was crucified. Jesus died because it was part of the plan of God. Jesus died because of everyone's sin, including your sin and mine. We made Jesus die because we sin, and we like to sin. That causes God great pain. He loves us, and he wants us to be as pure as he is, but our sin is so great that we cannot live with him the way we are. Jesus took our punishment for us and forgave us our sins. That is the reason Jesus died.

Being a follower of Jesus means that we know all of this, and we want to tell everyone else in the world how good Jesus was to all of us. We want everyone to know that sin is bad, and that Jesus died for our sins. But people do not want to be told by others how good God is, and how bad their sin is. They don't always like followers of Jesus. You may find some people who do not like you because you are a Christian who loves God. It will hurt you to know that these people do not like you and want you to stay away from them. It would be easy to live by ourselves and never go near these people, but we can't. We are followers of Jesus, and because we follow him, we must do what is right and share the love of God with everyone. That is the reason Jesus said each of us would have to carry a cross, just as he did. We may not die the way He did, nailed to a cross, but we will find people who will hate us because we are followers of Jesus. That's all right. It is going to happen. But we will keep loving even the people who hate us because that is the way Jesus taught us.

I have a small cross for each of you to take home and keep to remind us that we are followers of Jesus, and that we will follow him in times of trouble just as we do in the good times. Amen.

On The Lookout

Mark 13:33-37

Keep a sharp lookout! For you do not know when I will come, at evening, at midnight, early dawn or late daybreak. Don't let me find you sleeping. Watch for my return! This is my message to you and to everyone else. (vv. 35-37)

Object: Binoculars

Good morning, boys and girls. Have you ever kept the watch? I mean, has anyone ever asked you to do nothing but look out for someone else who was supposed to come? The cowboys used to keep a lookout for Indians with binoculars and the Indians used to keep a lookout for the cowboys. They didn't trust each other, so they would have a couple of people stay up at night and watch to make sure that no one would sneak up on them. The army has lookouts for the same reason. If you were in the army you would have to take your turn watching with binoculars for the enemy. If you were in the navy you would have to stand on the highest part of the shop with your binoculars so that you could watch for submarines or airplanes or whatever else may come near the ship.

Keeping watch is something that we used to do a lot more than we do now. But not too many years ago it was very important to have warnings when certain things were going to happen. Today we have a radar and things like that to warn us of danger.

Jesus also thought that it was important that we had a lookout. Only this lookout was not for an enemy, but for him. Jesus wanted Christians to be alert and to watch for him when he returned. If we were watching for him, that would mean that we were alert and doing the kind of things that were good for us. When we stop watching, we also stop thinking, and Jesus knew how easy it would be for us to stop thinking about him and God his Father when he was gone.

Jesus is coming back to earth. That is a promise that he made to every one of us. It could be tomorrow, or it could be a hundred or thousand years from now. We don't know when he is coming, and he didn't tell us. The only thing that Jesus said was that we should be alert, and keep a watch out so that when he came we would be ready.

If we check on our watchout, then we will be thinking about Jesus. When we think about Jesus, we are living the way God wants us to live.

I don't think we need to stand on the tallest building with binoculars looking for Jesus, but I do think that we should look in our hearts to make sure that our lives are ready for him when he comes. Remember his teachings, share his love with others, and worship the Father in heaven. Then we will be ready for Jesus the moment he arrives. Amen.

Congratulations!

Luke 1:26-38

*Gabriel appeared to her and said, "Congratulations, favored lady!
The Lord is with you." (v. 28)*

**Objects: The word CONGRATULATIONS spelled out in large let-
ters on a big piece of paper or a roll of paper that can be held by
two children.**

Good morning, boys and girls. Today I brought a big sign
with me and I need some volunteers to help hold it up. (Select
the children and let them unroll it until everyone can see the
big sign.) How many of you know what the word means that
you see spelled out in front of you. (Let them read it.) CON-
GRATULATIONS! What does that mean? If someone said to
you, CONGRATULATIONS, what do you think they would be
telling you? (Let them answer.) That's right, it means that you
did something terrific and others want you to know that they
like what you did. Can you think of something that you did
that other people might say, "Congratulations," to you? (Let
them answer.)

The Bible tells us that an angel once said, "CON-
GRATULATIONS," to Mary. Why do you think an angel would
say that to Mary? (Let them answer.) Those are pretty good
answers, but let me tell you the whole story. Mary was just
a very young woman and not even married when the angel
Gabriel visited her. She was a little frightened, but Gabriel
told her not to worry because he had good news. I don't think

that Mary had ever seen an angel before. Have any of you seen an angel? Most people have never seen an angel, but this time one came to visit Mary. Gabriel said, "CONGRATULATIONS, FAVORED LADY!" Then Gabriel told her that she had been chosen by God to have a baby, a very special baby. Well, Mary knew that she was not married, and that only married people were supposed to have babies and she told the angel what she believed. Gabriel knew that Mary would feel like that and he told her this was something very special since she had been chosen by God to have his Son.

It was special. We all know how special Jesus was now, but then it was pretty frightening. But Mary trusted in God and soon her fear went away.

It isn't often that we are congratulated by an angel who was bringing a message from God. That must have really been something.

The next time that you hear someone say, "CONGRATULATIONS," I hope you remember the day that the angel of God said that word to Mary and how he told her that she was going to have the special baby named Jesus. Amen.

Dedication Time

Luke 2:20-40

For in these laws God had said, "If a woman's first child is a boy, he should be dedicated to the Lord." (v. 23)

Objects: *A piece of bright ribbon and a scissors.*

Good morning, boys and girls. How many of you have ever been to a store when they had a grand opening? (Let them answer.) Have you ever been to a special ceremony for a new church or school? (Let them answer.) A big time like this is called a dedication. Usually the people who own the store or build the building put a bright ribbon across the door, and then at just the right time in the ceremony someone cuts the ribbon with a pair of brand new scissors.

Let's pretend that we are opening a new store and that all of you have come to see it. I will be the speaker, one of you can be the owner who cuts the ribbon, and the rest of you can be the happy people who have come to shop. (Have two children hold the ribbon and then proceed to give a small speech about how happy you are that everyone has come and that this store is being dedicated to all the shoppers in town who want good food and low prices. Emphasize the dedication of the building to the people.) Now we cut the ribbon and the store is officially open. Wasn't that fun? A dedication is always a great occasion because it makes everyone feel good. The people feel good because the store of building is dedicated to giving them good service, and the owner is happy because he has a better place and a way to serve the people.

I have shared all of this with you because I want to talk to you about the time when the parents of Jesus dedicated him to God. He was the first born son in a Jewish family, and all first born sons were dedicated to God. That is the way God said it should be, and the people did as God said because they knew it made everyone happy. Mary and Joseph brought Jesus to the temple in Jerusalem and they had a great ceremony dedicating Jesus to Almighty God. There were some speeches, some singing, and some special readings in the great temple as they dedicated a child to the service of God.

I can tell you that Mary and Joseph were very happy people. Others who were there were also happy, and two people by the name of Simeon and Anna even believed that they recognized Jesus as the Savior of the world. It was a great day. They did not cut any ribbons or say nice things about the building, but on this day they dedicated the baby Jesus to the service of God.

Thank you for coming to share with me, and remember that God loves you. Amen.

We Saw It Coming

Luke 24:13-35

Wasn't it clearly predicted by the prophets that the Messiah would have to suffer all these things before entering His time of glory?" (v. 26)

Object: *A crystal ball.*

Good morning, boys and girls. How many of you know what it means to predict? Do you know what the word predict means? (Let them answer.) That's right, it means that you can tell something that is going to happen before it happens. I can predict that your arm is going to hurt before I hit it with my fist. I know that, and I can tell you that before I do it. It is kind of easy to make that kind of a prediction since I am the one who is doing it, and I know what an arm that has been hit feels like because it has happened to me.

Some people believe that they can predict what is going to happen to others by looking into a crystal ball. (Show the crystal ball.) How many of you think that you could predict what is going to happen to other people by staring into this crystal ball? (Let them answer.) Would someone like to try it? (See if you can get someone to look into the ball. If you do, then set a very mysterious mood for the other children.) My, that does sound mysterious, doesn't it? How many of you believe that our friend has predicted the future? No one. I agree with you.

But now I want to tell you about some other predictions that did come true. Did you know that hundreds and even thousands of years before Jesus as born on this earth, there were prophets who predicted that Jessus would have to suffer the way he did and even die in the way he did before he was resurrected from the grave? Did you know that the prophets predicted almost everything that happened? It's true. Do you think that they used a crystal ball? (Let them answer.) You are right. They did not use a crystal ball. The kind of predictions they made did not come from crystal balls or anything like them, but instead they came because they listened closely to God. God wanted men to know that he was sending Jesus as a Savior. God also wanted men to know that he took our sins very seriously and wanted to change our world and the way we lived. That is why God told the prophets, so that they could tell the rest of the world.

When Jesus suffered and died it was no surprise, but part of the plan of God. The prophets predicted what was going to happen, but they didn't use a crystal ball. They used prayer and quiet conversation with God in heaven. Jesus died and came back to life, but it was all part of God's plan to show us how much he loved us and how much he wants us to be a part of his way of living and his world. You can share that life by knowing how much God loves you.

God bless you. Amen.

Standing Up For Jesus

John 1:1-18

God sent John the Baptist as a witness to the fact that Jesus Christ is the true light. (vv. 6-7)

Object: An important document like a wedding certificate or another document that requires the signature of a witness.

Good morning, boys and girls. How many of you know what a witness is? (Let them answer.) That's good. Most of you have heard the word and you know how to use it. For instance, there are some things which require a witness to sign a paper before it is legal. I have some very important papers here with me that have a line at the bottom for someone called a witness to sign. (Show them the documents.)

The paper document like this wedding license or this business paper, called a contract, is for someone else, but the witness says that he was there at the time that the agreement was made. For instance, when two people get married, there is a place for the minister to sign the wedding paper, and also a place for the best man and the maid of honor to sign their names as witnesses. The witnesses did not get married, but they signed the paper so that if anyone ever questions the marriage, they can say that they were there and they saw these two people get married. They are witnesses.

God wanted a witness to announce to the world that Jesus was his son. He had a witness whose name was John. We call him John the Baptist, and he was a witness for Jesus. God had shown John that this Jesus was the Son, the Savior.

God meant for John to tell what he knew to other people. There was a time when some of the men who were followers of John were present when Jesus passed by. John told them that Jesus was the true light, which meant that Jesus was the Son of God. He told them so that they would listen carefully to everything Jesus said, for they might have the chance to be a disciple of Jesus.

That is exactly what happened to some of the followers of John. They did become disciples of Jesus. But John was the witness. He was the one who pointed Jesus out to others and said that God had told him all of the wonderful things that Jesus was going to do, and they should follow this true light wherever he would lead them.

Being a witness is a very important position. A witness tells the truth about what he saw happen, or what he heard said. Someday you may be a witness to something very important, and then you will understand the tremendous responsibility you have to tell the truth. It was John's responsibility to tell what he saw and knew about Jesus.

God bless you. Amen.

You're Invited

John 1:29-41

"Come and see," he said. So they went with him to the place where he was staying and were with him from about four o'clock that afternoon until the evening. (v. 39)

Object: *An invitation (wedding, open house, party).*

Good morning, boys and girls. How many of you have been invited to a party? Did you get an invitation to the party in the mail? Sometimes people send invitations to their parties. Have you ever seen a wedding invitation? When two people are going to get married, the parents of the bride and groom send out invitations to all of their friends to come to the wedding. Maybe you have been invited to someone's new house, or to a school play, or even to a friend's church. When your friend invites you by letter or on the telephone, he is telling you that he wants to share something that he is going to do with you. I think being invited by a friend to do something with him is a wonderful experience.

Jesus used to invite people to share things with him, and they always loved to be with him. One day two disciples of John the Baptist saw Jesus walk by and they followed him. They had heard so many wonderful things about him that they were a little afraid to just go up and speak to him, so they decided to walk behind him and see where he went. It wasn't long before Jesus knew that he was being followed. He turned and asked the two men what they wanted. The two men were embarrassed and didn't know what to say. Finally one of them blurted out that they just wondered where he lived. Jesus told them to follow him and they could see for themselves.

That was an invitation to join him, and they hurried to catch up with him. That was the beginning of one of the most wonderful days of their lives. They spent the day from 4:00 in the afternoon until the evening with Jesus. They asked him questions and even told him how they felt about some things. They loved Jesus and they knew that he was something really special. What a wonderful time that must have been! Just think how you would feel if you could spend an afternoon with Jesus. Doesn't that sound great!

I suppose that you can spend time with Jesus in a little different way. I hope that you save some time to pray and talk over any problems that you might have with Jesus. I know a lot of people who do. They save some time in the early morning or before they go to bed to just sit down and talk things over with Jesus like a good friend. Jesus invites you to do it, too. Why don't you give it a try?

God bless you. Amen.

Better Than We Think

John 1:43-51

"Nazareth!" exclaimed Nathanael. "Can anything good come from there?" "Just come and see for yourself," Philip declared. (v. 46)

Objects: *Some mold and a penicillin tablet.*

Good morning, boys and girls. How many of you have ever thought that something good could come from something not so good? Let me ask you another way. How many of you like mold? Can anything good come from something that is moldy? (Let them answer.) You don't think that something moldy will make something good. Suppose I told you that some kinds of mold make the best medicine in the world, and that if it were not for mold, many people would die. What would you think of that? (Let them answer.) That's right. Scientists make penicillin out of mold. How many of you have ever had a penicillin shot or a penicillin tablet that helped make you well when you were pretty sick? (Let them answer.) A lot of you have had the experience.

The reason I told you this is that something like it happened to one of the disciples one day. You rememer that Jesus grew up in a town called Nazareth. It was a small town, really a tiny village, and not many people even knew that it existed. Some may have heard about it, but few people knew where it was or knew anybody who lived there. It was just a quiet little village, where mostly poor people lived. One day, after Jesus had asked a few men to follow him including a man called Philip, the disciples and Jesus were traveling from one town to another. While they were walking, Philip saw a man whom he knew. The man's name was Nathanael or Bartholomew. He was the same man, but some people knew him by one name and others knew him by his other name. Philip was really excited about Jesus and wanted to share his feelings with his friend Bartholomew. He told him almost everything he knew and even invited Bartholomew to meet Jesus. Do you know what Bartholomew said? (Let them answer.) Bartholomew looked at Philip and then he said this, "Can anything good come from Nazareth?" It was like you or me saying, "Can anything good come from mold?" If we don't know the right answer, sometimes we ask a dumb question. That's what Bartholomew did and I know that he never forgot it.

Well, we know the answer today. Of course, something good can come out of Nazareth. The very best "good" in the whole world came out of Nazareth and no one has ever forgotten it.

Maybe the next time you see something you don't think is so good, like some mold on bread or cheese, you will remember the story about Bartholomew and the day he asked a dumb question about Jesus. But, I want you also to know that Bartholomew changed his mind and became a disciple of Christ and followed Jesus forever. Amen.

Which One's Real?

John 4:5-26

*For it's not where we worship that counts, but how we worship
— is our worship spiritual and real? Do we have the Holy Spirit's
help? (v. 23)*

Objects: *Some imitation fruit and some real fruit.*

Good morning, boys and girls. Today we are going to talk
about the way that we worship God. We want to ask ourselves
if our worship is real or is it just something we do to make
ourselves feel good? Let me show you what I mean.

I have two bowls of fruit. They are beautiful and they make
my mouth water just looking at them. How many of you like
fruit? (Let them answer.) Apples, oranges, pears, and bananas
are my favorites. I could eat one of them every hour of the
day. If you had your choice of a piece of fruit, which one would
you like? (Let them choose. As they choose a piece of fruit,
pass it out to them.) How many of you like the piece of fruit
that I gave you? Please don't eat it in church, but as soon
as you get outside take a big bite of your favorite fruit and
remember who gave it to you. (As some of the children
discover that they have imitation fruit and begin to tell you
about it, bring your discussion to an end and deal with the
fact that everything is not real.)

Does it make a difference that it is not real fruit? I know
that you can't eat it, but that helps it to last longer. It never
spoils, it shines up beautifully and once you have a good looking banana you never need another one. I know that it isn't

the same, but does it really make that much difference? (Let them answer.)

Of course it makes a difference. There is a big difference between something that is real and something that is not real. The reason that we have talked about this is because I want to show you that it makes a difference not only with fruit, but with a lot of things. One thing that makes a big difference is with worship. When you worship God you want to worship in the real way. You want to know that the Spirit of God is helping you.

There are some people who want worship to be beautiful, or to be soft, or loud, or with only organ music, or with no music, or in the morning, or in the afternoon. In other words people like the things ABOUT worship, but they do not really care TO worship. Jesus knew that and he told it to a lady one day who talked about worshiping God on a certain mountain. Jesus told the woman that the place did not make worship real, but having the Spirit of God helping you made it real. The place is not important, and neither is anything else. The most important thing is being real. If you want to eat an apple or a pear, you need the real fruit. If you want to worship God you need the real Spirit and nothing else will take his place.

Thank you very much for sharing with me this morning, and remember that God loves you always. Amen.

Look At Both Sides

John 9:13-17, 34-39

Some of them said, "Then this fellow Jesus is not from God, because he is working on the Sabbath." Others said, "But how could an ordinary sinner do such miracles?" So there was deep division of opinion among them. (v. 16)

Object: Shampoo

Good morning, boys and girls. How many of you have ever had a disagreement with one of your friends? (Let them answer.) All of us have our own opinions, and we don't always agree with one another. For instance, how many of you like to wash your hair? (Take out the shampoo.) How many of you think it's fun to put a little bit of this on your hair and rub your head until it's all fluffy and white? (Let them answer.) When you are finished, your hair smells good and clean, and maybe it is even a few pounds lighter. That is a great feeling.

How many of you don't like to wash your hair? A shampoo gives you a good feeling unless you are one of those people who gets soap in your eyes every time your head is shampooed. Then it is awful. You know what I mean. The soap runs in your eyes, and your eyes burn until there are tears, and you can't find the towel, and when you do, you drop it in the tub, and you are already mad because you didn't want to wash your head in the first place. How many of you feel like that? (Let them answer.) Right, that is an awful feeling.

There are two sides to the question. It isn't easy to like washing your hair if you just don't like it, and it is not easy to understand people who don't like to wash their hair if you like to.

It was one of those kinds of days for Jesus when he healed someone on the Sabbath day. People felt differently about it. Some people thought it was terrible that Jesus was working on the Sabbath. They didn't believe that he could be from God and do that kind of thing. Other people thought that Jesus must be special to God because an ordinary person could never do the things that Jesus did. People argued about it for hours. Some said that Jesus was from God, and other people said that he was from the devil. You know how it is when people make up their minds. The more they argue for one side, the surer they are that they are on the right side. Jesus knew how confused the people were when they heard those arguments. The leaders were so angry that they threw the man Jesus healed out of the temple because he told them how much Jesus had helped him. But Jesus would not stand for that, so he told the man something that only a few people knew at that time. He told him that he had been healed by the chosen one of God. He also told those who called him evil how wrong they were to tell people that he was evil and they would be punished for not teaching the truth.

It is not bad to have opinions and to disagree, but when you find out that you are wrong, you should admit it and then do whatever is right. That is what Jesus told the people, and it is something for you to remember when you think about how much God loves you.

What's A Door For?

John 10:1-10

Yes, I am the Gate. Those who come in by way of the Gate will be saved and will go in and out and find green pastures. (v. 9)

Object: A doorknob.

Good morning, boys and girls. I brought with me this morning a small part of every house that is very important to all of us. People who use it are our friends, and people who come into our house and do not use it are usually not our friends. Can anyone guess what it is? (Let them guess.) That is a pretty difficult riddle. Let me show you what I brought along. (Take out the doorknob.) Now you know what I mean. This is a doorknob without the door. Almost every door has one of these, and it is the thing that helps us to open and close the door. People who use this way to come and go from our homes are our friends. If a person gets into our house and does not come in the door, then he is usually up to no good. How else can people get into your house? (Let them answer.) That's right, they can climb in open windows, or break the window, but what does that mean? That means that they are not welcome, and they have come to steal or at least to get into our house when they are not welcome. People who do that are wrong and cause harm and danger.

Jesus talked about something like that when he said that he was the Gate. That was a way of telling people that anyone who wanted to be a part of God's world would have to know him and believe in him before he could get in. The gate that

Jesus was talking about was the gate that sheep would go in at night, and out of in the morning. When the sheep went in the gate, they were safe and when they went out the gate they were safe, because the shepherd went with them. If a wolf came, he never came in the gate, but he would try to jump over the fence at some place where the shepherd could not see him. But the fence was high and the sheep could feel safe inside of the gate.

Jesus said that he was the Gate and that anyone who came to God through him would be safe and never have to worry about anything. If you were a sheep it would make you very happy to know that there was a gate to the place where you stayed. You are also very glad to know that you have a strong door on your house that lets you go in and out, but keeps everyone else away who doesn't belong or is not invited.

Jesus is the way to know God and to believe in his promises. That is why he called himself the Gate and we are thrilled to know that he watches over all of his believers and keeps us safe from any evil.

God bless you. Amen.

Feelings That Match

John 11:35-36

Tears came to Jesus' eyes. "They were close friends," the Jewish leaders said. "See how much he loved him." (vv. 35-36)

Objects: Some things that match, such as earrings, mittens, gloves, or a suit coat and suit pants.

Good morning, boys and girls. Today we are going to talk about love in a little different way than we often do. I am reminded of love when I read the story in the Bible about the time that Jesus' friend Lazarus died and Jesus cried because he loved him. It is hard for us to think about Jesus crying since he was God, and whatever God wants, he can have. At least that is the way most people understand God. If you were God or I was God, we might see to it that we made things work out our own way, but that is not the way God is, or the way he does things.

Love is God, and God is love. They are a perfect match. Love always matches whatever it loves. Let me show you what I mean. Here is an earring. It has a certain shape, certain color, and is worn in a certain place. (Now show them the other objects that match and also the matching earring.) Can you pick out the object that matches what I have in my hand? That's very good! I am sure that you will be able to match the other objects that I have with these pieces. They belong together.

The same thing is true with love and the objects of our love. For instance, when you are happy, the people who love you are happy. When you are sad, the people who love you are sad. That is the way it is with you and me, and that is the way it is with God, too.

The reason that I know that this is true is because Jesus was like this many times. One time was when Lazarus died. Jesus knew that Lazarus was all right and that he would have a full life in heaven, but he also was sorry for all of the people, including himself, who would miss Lazarus here on earth. The Bible says that Jesus cried. There were tears in his eyes.

I am not glad that Lazarus died, but I am glad to know that God feels as we feel. His feelings match our feelings. You remember how the earrings and clothes matched each other. So do our feelings and God's feelings match each other. When we are happy, God is happy for us; and when we feel great sorrow, then God also feels sorrow with us.

It is good to know that God has feelings and shares these feelings with us. I hope that the next time you see something that matches you will remember that God's feelings match our feelings and also that God loves you.

God bless you. Amen.

Better Things Coming

John 12:20-33

*"Jesus replied that the time had come for him to return to his
glory in heaven and that, 'I must fall and die like a kernel of wheat
that falls into the furrows of the earth. Unless I die I will be alone
— a single seed. But my death will produce many new wheat kernels
— a plentiful harvest of new lives.' " (vv. 23-24)*

**Object: *Some wheat, enough to pass out to all of the children
present.***

Good morning, boys and girls. How many of you have ever
held any wheat? (Let them answer.) Some of you have and
some of you have not. I brought some wheat with me this
morning and I want each of you to have one kernel of wheat
to hold in your hand. I want you to think about the wheat while
I ask you some questions. Suppose you take that kernel of
wheat and put it on your dresser at home. What will happen
to it? (Let them answer.) If you do not lose it, the answer that
I heard when someone said "nothing," is correct. Nothing will
happen to it. It will just lay there and rot. Suppose you take
the same piece of wheat and put it into the ground and bury
it. What will happen to it then? (Let them answer.) That's right,
it will grow and make a plant. Did you know that it had to die
first when you put it into the ground and bury it? Did you know
that one wheat seed put into the ground will make hundreds
of new wheat seeds when the plant grows? If you didn't know
that before, you know it now and you also know what Jesus
meant when he compared himself to a wheat seed.

Jesus told his disciples that he had to die if the lives of every person were to be better. Jesus knew that he had to die and while all of his disciples said, "No, no, we don't want you to die," Jesus knew that he must if we were going to live forever. Jesus shows us that dying for men was like a kernel of wheat dying. If we continue to live here on earth like we are living now, we will just grow old and never have anything better. But Jesus said that if we die like the kernel of wheat it will be a hundred times better than it is now.

Some of us are afraid of dying. We are not sure where we are going or what is going to happen to us after we die. If we believe Jesus, and we should, then we know that it is going to be wonderful and at least a hundred times better than it is today. That is a real promise and one that we should never forget. If we believe Jesus, then we will not worry about dying, but instead, just enjoy the life that he gave us to live here on earth until God is ready to give us the hundred times better life that we are going to have in the future.

Just Like His Father

John 14:1-12

Don't you believe that I am in the Father and the Father is in me? The words I say are not my own but are from my Father who lives in me. And He does His work through me. (v. 10)

Objects: Some Spic and Span, some warm water in a bucket, and some dirty painted wood.

Good morning, boys and girls. How many of you ever thought that Jesus could be like Spic and Span? Do you know what I mean when I say Spic and Span? It is the name of a cleaner your mother uses when she wants to wash some woodwork or furniture that is dirty. She puts the Spic and Span into a bucket of warm water and swishes it around. Then with a sponge she washes the piece of furniture. Before you know it, the wood is clean as can be. Once you put the Spic and Span in the warm water, you cannot see it. The water and the Spic and Span go together to make a very powerful cleaner.

Jesus talked about the Father in heaven and himself as being the same way. One lived inside of the other, and you could not tell them apart. When Jesus talked, it was the Father talking. When Jesus worked, it was the Father working. One could not be separated from the other. Some people think that they can separate Jesus from the Father and tell you what each one does. Jesus says that this is not true. The Father spoke through Jesus and worked through Jesus.

If you were to look for the green powder that I put into

the water to wash the wood, you would not be able to find it. It has disappeared into the water. It would be hard to pick out some water that does not have the green powder in it, because it has become partly Spic and Span. Both of them together work hard to make things clean. The same thing is true of God the Father and God the Son. They work together and speak together so that we might be saved from our sin and live forever in heaven. This is a realy happy thought for all believers.

The next time that you see your mother clean with Spic and Span or something like it in water you can remember the time that I told you how Jesus and the Father go together in the same way. When Jesus speaks, it is the Father speaking through him, and when he works it is the Father working through him. No wonder we are so sure of God's love for us. I want you to remember how much God loves you and share some of his love with someone else today. Will you do that? That's wonderful.

God bless you. Amen.

What's the Result?

John 14:15-21

The one who obeys me is the one who loves me; and because he loves me, my Father will love him; and I will too, and I will reveal myself to him. (v. 21)

Object: *A watch.*

Good morning, boys and girls. Today we are going to talk about results. Do you know what the word "result" means? (Let them answer.) The word "result" is what happened because of something else. When you do something, you get results. If you eat too much, the result will be that you might get too fat. Do you understand now? Let me show you what I mean.

Here is a watch. It is a beautiful watch. A watch has a very special purpose. It wasn't made just for beauty, was it? No, it was made to tell time. Now if I am going to have the right time, I must do something to my watch every day. Do you know what that something is? (Let them answer.) That's right, I must wind it. When I wind my watch, I get results. My watch keeps time and that is the purpose of the watch.

That was a very good lesson because it also will help us to learn something about God. The Bible teaches us that if we obey the teaching of Jesus, it means also that we love Jesus. If we obey, then we have good results. Jesus taught us about the way we should live, such as loving our enemies, visiting the sick, helping the poor, sharing the things we have with people who do not have as much as we do. If we do those things, and more, it is a sign that we love Jesus. That is kind of like winding the watch. What happens when we do them? Jesus says that God will love us and we will know it. That is like being able to tell the time of day from looking at our watch. That is a result.

We obey Jesus, and the result is that God will love us. Wind your watch and you will be able to tell time. Those are the results. That is what we are after.

The next time you see someone winding a watch or even looking to see the time of day, I hope you will think about Jesus and his love. You will remember the results that you can get by being obedient to Jesus. That's what it is all about. We all want good results, and the best results that I know are the love that comes from God and is shared with us.

God bless you. Amen.

Just Tell Me What You Want

John 17:1-11

For I have passed on to them the commands you gave me; and they accepted them and know of a certainty that I came down to earth from you, and they believe you sent me. (v. 8)

Objects: *Some restaurant menus, towel over arm and an order pad.*

Good morning, boys and girls. How many of you like to eat in a restaurant? Good, almost everyone likes to eat in a restaurant, so I know you will like to play this little game with me. I am going to pretend that I am your waiter, and you are going to be the people I am waiting on. You can order whatever you want from the menu, and I will take your order to the kitchen to have it prepared for you. (Pretend to take some orders by asking them what they would like and writing it down.) We certainly have a hungry group here this morning! I suppose you know the waiter does not do the cooking, and I know that you are aware that the waiter does not get to eat the food. The waiter is the person who takes the orders, but he is not the person who prepares the orders.

Jesus felt like he was a kind of waiter. He received his orders from God the Father and passed them on to the people here on earth. That was his job and he did it well. God the Father had certain ideas that he wanted to share with the people, but the Father needed someone who listened and understood what he said so he could tell it to the people. Just imagine what it would be like if everyone went into the cook and told him what he wanted to eat. It would be a mess. God did not want a mess. He had one messenger who took his commands and passed them on to the people so everyone understood exactly what God wanted.

The next time you go to a restaurant, I want you to notice the waiter and how careful he is to get everything just right. He may ask you several times what you want, because he knows that it is his job to see that the cook doesn't cook the wrong thing for you. Jesus was like that. He listened well and made sure that what God said was understood. Then he told the disciples and other people so they would know that these were not just the ideas of another man, but that they came from God.

The next time you go to a restaurant and you see a waiter, I want you to think about Jesus and how true he was to God the Father. When you think of Jesus, then you will know how true he was to God and to us, too.

God bless you. Amen.

Look for the Clues

John 20:1-9

We ran to the tomb to see; I outran Peter and got there first, and stopped and looked in and saw the linen cloth lying there, but I didn't go in. (vv. 3, 4)

Object: *Some fingerprints on a glass or mirror that can be easily seen.*

Good morning, boys and girls, and Happy Easter! Isn't this a day like no other day in your life! Easter, what a great day it is for everyone who believes that God cares and wants us to live with him forever. Easter is the day when the problem was solved. There had been a lot of clues before then, but that was the day when the case was solved. It sounds like I am a private detective, doesn't it? Clues, cases solved, and evidence. I guess you can say that is the way I feel.

Let me tell you a little story about what happened on the day of Jesus' resurrection. Do you remember how the women had come to the place where Jesus was buried and found out that the tomb stone had been rolled away? The angel told them that Jesus was not there, but that he was risen from the dead. You remember that, don't you? The rolled away stone was a piece of evidence, or a clue that something had happened. It is kind of like a fingerprint on a glass or a mirror. (Show them the glass or mirror and point out the fingerprint.)

Well, when the women ran back to town and told Peter and John, the disciples, you can imagine how excited they were to see for themselves. They ran to the tomb. John was a lot younger and a lot faster, and he got there first. When he looked inside the tomb, he saw another clue that the women had not seen. When a person was buried in those days, a piece of cloth that looked like a napkin was laid over the face. That is just the way it was done. When John looked inside the tomb, he saw the piece of cloth lying there. It wasn't covering anyone's face. John knew that something had happened. It was another clue like another fingerprint.

John didn't go inside the tomb. He waited for Peter, but he must have been thinking to himself that something pretty strange and wonderful was happening. John had to think about the things that Jesus said before he died. He could remember how Jesus promised that after three days of death he would rise and come back to life. Here was another clue, just like another fingerprint. Jesus promised that it would happen, and he told them how long it would take for it to happen.

Well, when you have enough clues, you have some evidence to make a case and even solve it. The disciples began to think that Jesus was alive even before they saw him. There were real clues to suggest that God had made the greatest victory of all happen. God had conquered death for all of us. That's why he did it, to save us all and share his love. When you have a clue like a fingerprint, you can remember the day that John saw the face napkin and started solving the mystery called Easter.

Behind Locked Doors

John 20:19-23

That evening the disciples were meeting behind locked doors, in fear of the Jewish leaders; when suddenly Jesus was standing there among them. (v. 19)

Objects: *Some various kinds of locks.*

Good morning, boys and girls. What do you do when you are frightened? (Let them answer.) Do you hide? Do you put your head under the pillow? Do you find someone who is not frightened, like your mom or dad, or what do you do? Did I ever tell you about the time when the disciples of Jesus were frightened because they thought that the people who crucified Jesus were looking for them? They thought that if they were caught they would be crucified also. That would scare anyone. What do you think that they did?

I'll show you what they did. They locked themselves in their rooms and hid during the daytime so that no one could find them. I think a lock makes us believe that we are safe. I see a lot of things that people keep locked up so no one can take them or find them. I see bicycles locked up, cars locked up, boxes locked up and, of course, houses locked up. Locks are meant to keep certain things in and certain things out. When I lock my house I want to keep all of the things that I think belong to me inside, and I want to keep people who might take those things from getting inside and taking them. That is the reason I lock my house.

The disciples locked the house they stayed in so that the

people who were looking for them could not find them, and if they did, they could not get in to get them. The doors were locked tight, says the Bible. The disciples felt pretty safe.

But in spite of the fact that all of the locks were on, the disciples looked up one day and there was Jesus standing before them. He had walked right through the door. He didn't open the door or sneak in when no one was looking. He just walked through the door. Of course, this happened after he was resurrected from the dead and his body was something very special, but still it was a real miracle that no one there ever understood. But Jesus did not come to see the disciples to show them how he could walk through doors. He came to share the good news that the disciples could now forgive sins with the power of the Holy Spirit. That is what Jesus came to tell them, and it is something that none of us will ever forget. The power of God is great; it can even get through locked doors. But the real power is the power of love that God shares through the Holy Spirit.

God bless you. Amen.

Here's Proof!

John 20:24-31

Then He said to Thomas, "Put your finger into my hands. Put your hand into my side. Don't be faithless any longer. Believe!" (v. 27)

Objects: An x-ray, a laboratory slide.

Good morning, boys and girls. Today we are going to talk about believing. How many of you believe in something? (Let them answer.) Do you know what I mean when I say "believe?" (Let them answer.) It sounds kind of hard, doesn't it? How many of you believe that your mother loves you? (Let them answer.) All of you believe that. Why do you believe that your mother loves you? Can you prove that she loves you? (Let them answer.) It is hard to prove love, but you are positive that mothers love their children.

Sometimes a doctor tells one of his patients that he believes that there is something wrong with the patient's body. That is what the doctor believes, but that isn't good enough for everybody, including the doctor. A doctor always tries to prove his belief to the patient and to himself. Sometimes a doctor believes that there is nothing wrong with the patient, but the patient doesn't feel right, and so he doesn't believe the doctor when he tells him that he believes that he is all right. Do you know what a doctor does to prove whether a man is sick or not? (Let them answer.) The doctor gives the patient a lot of tests. (Hold up the x-ray and the slide.) Do you know what these are? That's right, these are some of the things that a doctor tests a patient with. He may take an x-ray, or a blood sample, or a lot of other tests to prove what is wrong or what is not wrong with his patient. Usually the patient will believe the doctor when he hears the results of his tests.

Jesus had a hard time making some people believe that he had really risen from the dead. A man by the name of Thomas was like that. He wanted to believe that Jesus was alive again, but he just could not believe what other people told him. Thomas said that he would have to put his finger into the place where the soldiers drove a nail through the hands or touch the side of Jesus where the soldier had thrown his spear.

Thomas needed to be shown that the person who said he was Jesus was the same Jesus who had died on the cross. He needed proof because he could not believe. Jesus gave that proof to Thomas when He showed him his hands and his side. Thomas believed when he saw the proof. You and I cannot see the wounds in Jesus' hands and side, but we must believe without seeing. We must believe that Jesus rose from the dead just as we believe that our mothers love us. We believe in something that cannot be proven today but what was proven to a man named Thomas a long time ago. When we believe in Jesus we share his love and his life forever.

God bless you. Amen.